To my own Miss Betty

My Honey

With Love

G-Lamb

Betty Bee said this to me.

I want to see what I can see.

I want to fly high as a kite!

Where the clouds clear away

to see the light.

I know I'm a bee and honey is my game,

But I think there is more . . .

let me explain.

I want some new and different friends.

I want new adventures

where fun never ends.

I want to meet others

who soar and fly

into the sky

way up high.

I want to ride on a pony's back

Galloping fast, clickity clack!

I want to play ball with a puppy,

and yarn with a cat.

I want more adventure,
so hold on to your hat!

I want to see swans,
lambs, and calves!

I want to see flowers,
streams
and winding paths!

I want to see oceans,

boats

and planes!

I want to ride bikes,

cars

and trains!

All of this I want to do,

But more than that,

I want to see you!

I want my family who touches the flowers

For the taste of honey,

both sweet and sour.

Yes, I buzz with excitement,

adventure and fun,

But there's nothing like family,

friends and the sun!

Betty Bee is my name,

flowers and honey are my game,

But I know what's important,

so I must explain . . .

Family,

love and friendship

mean more.

I'm glad we met,

so let's fly and soar!

About the Author:

Lyn lives in Southern California with her husband where they raised five children. They are now enjoying being grandparents.

Other books by the author include *Welcome with Wonder* and *The Monkey's Adventure.*

Design by Lyn Adelstein
www.lynadelstein.com

G-Lamb

32